STRINGSTASTIC
Level 1
DOUBLE BASS

By Lorraine Chai

STRINGSTASTIC

PO BOX 815 Epping NSW 1710 Australia
www.stringstastic.com
Copyright © 2023 Lorraine Chai

Book design by Meilisa Lengkong

All rights reserved.
Reproduction in whole or in part for any use whatsoever is strictly prohibited.

THE AUTHOR
LORRAINE CHAI

Lorraine is a multi-talented instrumentalist, international educator, and world-class coach. She graduated from the Sydney Conservatorium of Music with a Bachelor of Music Studies in 2008 and completed her Graduate Diploma of Education at the Australian Catholic University a year later. Lorraine also holds a Postgraduate Diploma in Education from Birmingham City University.

Having grown up in a musical family, Lorraine began piano lessons at the age of four and violin at the age of six, giving her first violin performance at just seven years of age. Lorraine started teaching violin at the age of 14 and founded a string ensemble at her local church. From there, teaching and performing became her passion.

Lorraine loves finding new and exciting ways students can learn their instrument in a classroom setting as well as in private lessons. Along with her musical journey and exposure to the various educational methods including Kodaly, Suzuki, Orff, and Dalcroze, Lorraine has also attended Alexander Technique workshops and has found that she can integrate these various methods into her own teaching technique for the benefit of her students.

Lorraine has an extensive ensemble and orchestral experience in Malaysia and Australia. Lorraine is currently the Music Director of Stringstastic Pty Ltd and is an active member of the Australian Strings Association, AUSTA NSW. She also co-ordinates instrumental programmes and runs string ensembles for some of Sydney's most celebrated schools.

PREFACE

This Stringstastic double bass book series is specifically designed for beginner bassists aged 6-12 years. Stringstastic Level 1 for double bass players introduces young players to the world of bass playing and music theory through games and fun graphics to assist the young bassists in better understanding the instrument and learning music theory in an enjoyable way.

This Stringstastic series can be used in a private lesson or alongside the violin, viola, and cello book series in a classroom setting.

For extra resources, go to www.stringstastic.com to download them for free.

Have fun!!

ACKNOWLEDGEMENT

This book was made possible with the encouragement of my family and loved ones. I would like to thank the following for their advice and input in making this book possible.

Dr. Rita Crews OAM, FMusA (honoris causa), PhD(UNE), BA(Hons), AMusTCL, FMusicolASMC, GradCertDistEd (UNE), HonFNMSM, DipMus (honoris causa) (AICM) MIMT, MACE, MMTA, JP.

Dr. Anthony Clarke DMA, MMus, Grad Dip, BMus Ed, DSCM, FTCL, LMusA, AMusA

Prof Barry Green BMus, MMus, renowned double bassist and educator, author of 3 double bass method books

Dr. h.c. Claus A. Freudenstein is an International double bass soloist and educator, founder of Freudenstein-Minibass and "The Bassmonsters", Artistic Director of "The Bavarian Bassdays", author

CONTENTS

4	STRING FAMILY
5	THE DOUBLE BASS PARTS
7	SIMON SAYS
8	TWO WAYS OF
9	MUSIC STAVE (STAFF)
11	BASS CLEF
13	DOUBLE BASS STRINGS
14	BAR LINES
15	READING NOTES
20	POSITION OF STEMS
23	NOTE VALUES
27	WHAT HAVE WE LEARNT SO FAR?
29	RESTS
31	TIME SIGNATURE
33	REVISION
35	ACCIDENTALS
38	D STRING
40	STRINGS AND NOTE NAMES
41	A STRING
43	REVISION D AND A STRING
45	G STRING
47	E STRING
49	REVISION (ON ALL STRINGS)
51	TEST

STRINGSTASTIC

String Family

Which is the smallest string instrument?

Which is the biggest string instrument?

Which instrument do you play?

Suzie and Tommy play in a string quartet. Suzie plays the smallest instrument while Tommy sits down playing his instrument.
Which instruments do Suzie and Tommy play?

Suzie:

Tommy:

Colour in Suzie and Tommy....

The Double Bass Parts

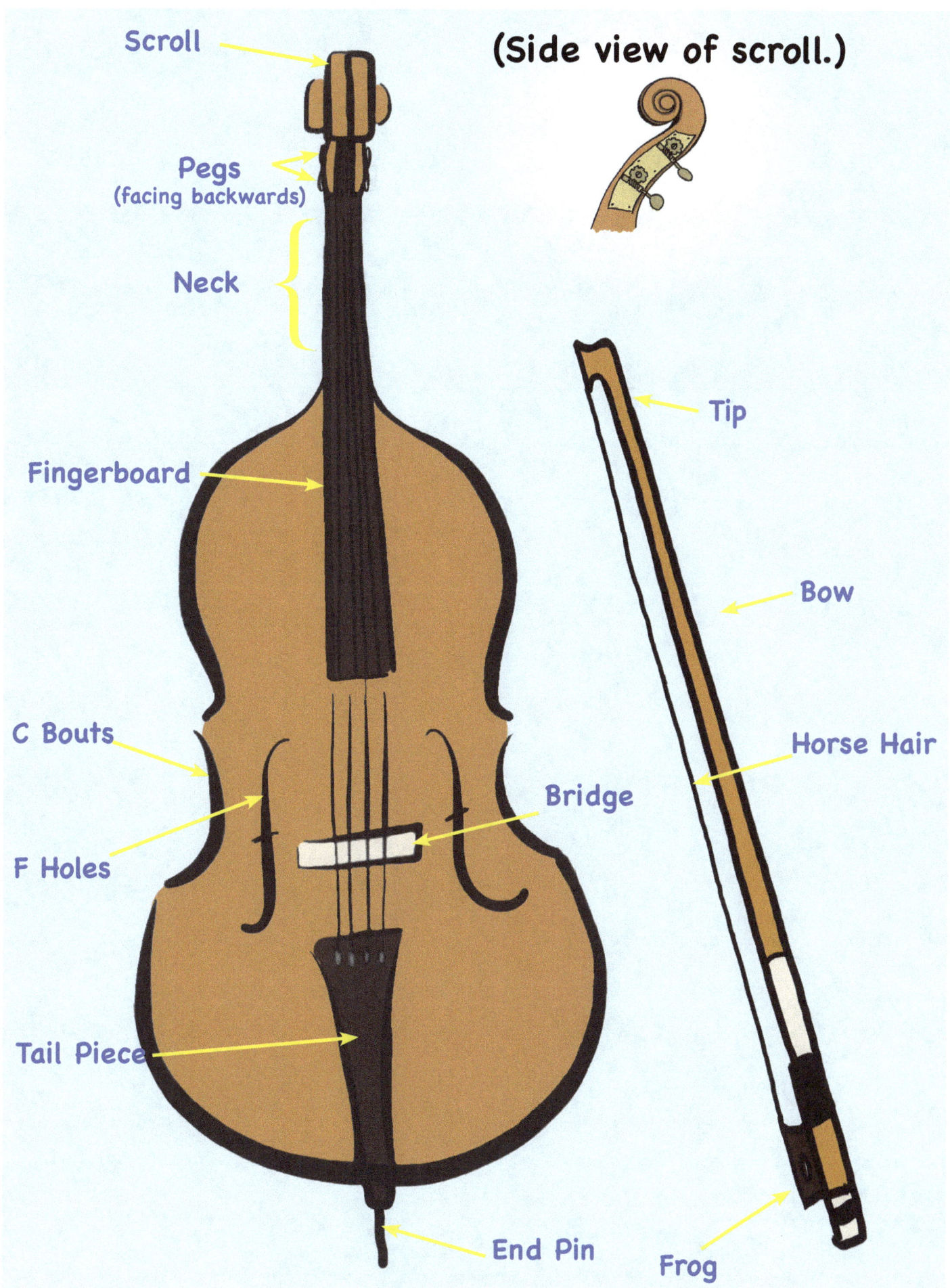

Draw the double bass and bow and label their parts.

Simon Says

Your teacher will give you the instructions. You are only allowed to move 5 times in this game. See how many movements you have made by the end of it.

Double Bass Placement (Standing)

1. Stand up nice and tall.

2. Hold the bass with your LEFT hand.

3. Straighten your LEFT arm and hold the bass on the end pin upright where the spine of the bass being in line with your LEFT FOOT.
(DON'T SQUEEZE THE BASS)

4. Turn the bass in a 45 degree angle facing inward.

5. Lean the upper right corner of the body to touch your belly button.

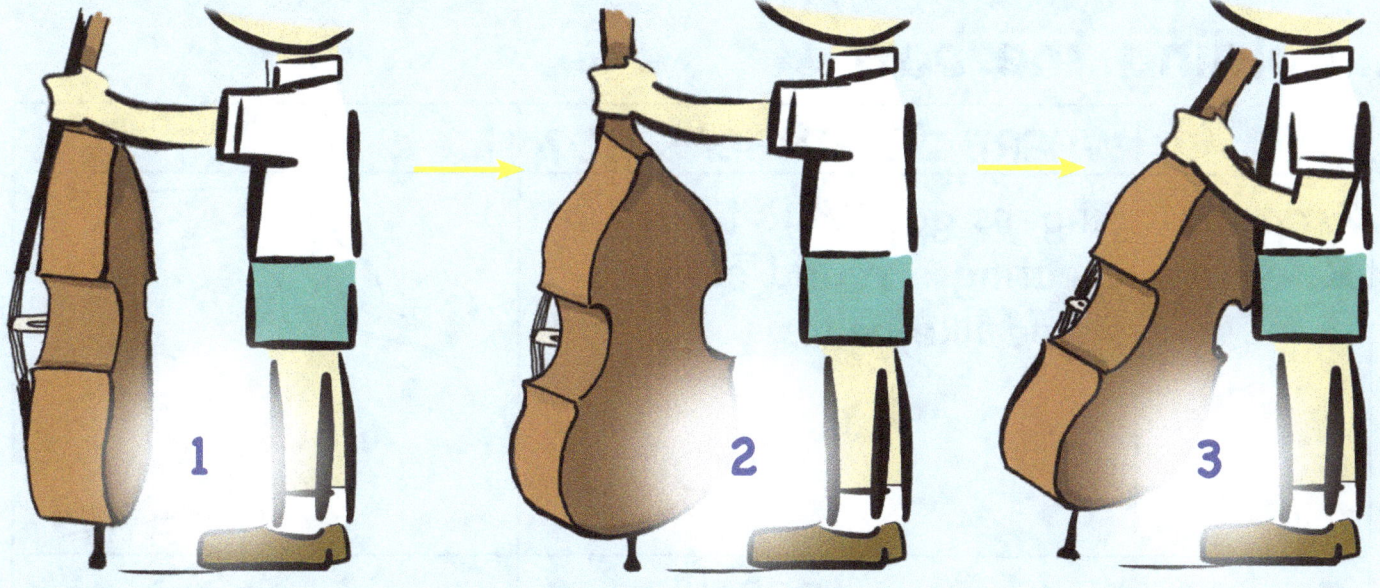

Double Bass Placement (Sitting)

The height of sitting is the same level as standing. Bass placement is the same as when standing.

Now let us see if you can teach mum or dad how to hold up the double bass. Could they do it as well you?

Two Ways of...

...playing the double bass

	MEANING	
arco	Pulling/pushing the bow across the string	
pizzicato or *pizz*	Plucking the string	

...holding the bow

	WHERE DO FINGERS GO?	
French Bow Hold	Fingers go OVER the frog creating a round curved shape like cello.	
German Bow Hold	Fingers go UNDER the frog with.	

Depending on your teacher, you may choose to learn one or both ways of holding the bow. They will talk you through in detail on the bow method.

Music Stave (Staff)

Music is written on these lines and spaces below.

Trace each line with the different colours and number each line from the bottom up.

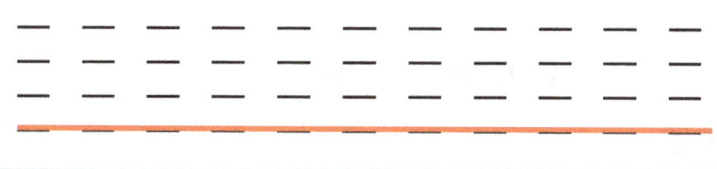

1. Red   2. Yellow   3. Blue   4. Green   5. Brown

How many lines does a stave have?

Draw a note through each line.

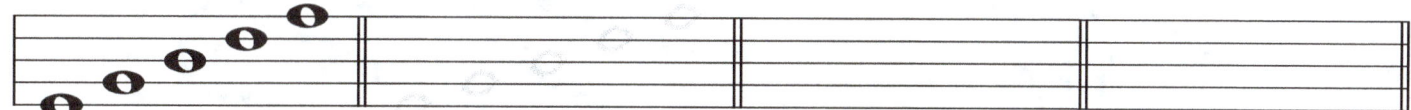

Colour each space with different colours and number the spaces.

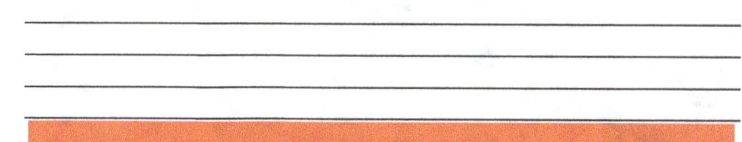

How many spaces does a stave have?

Draw a note in every space.

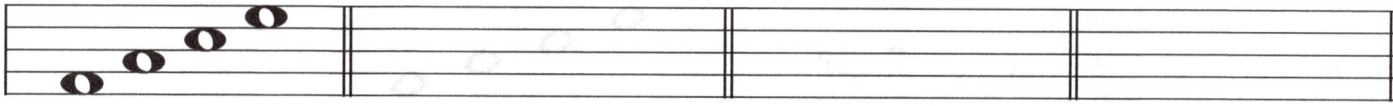

In the stave below, write an L below each note through a line and an S below each note in the spaces.

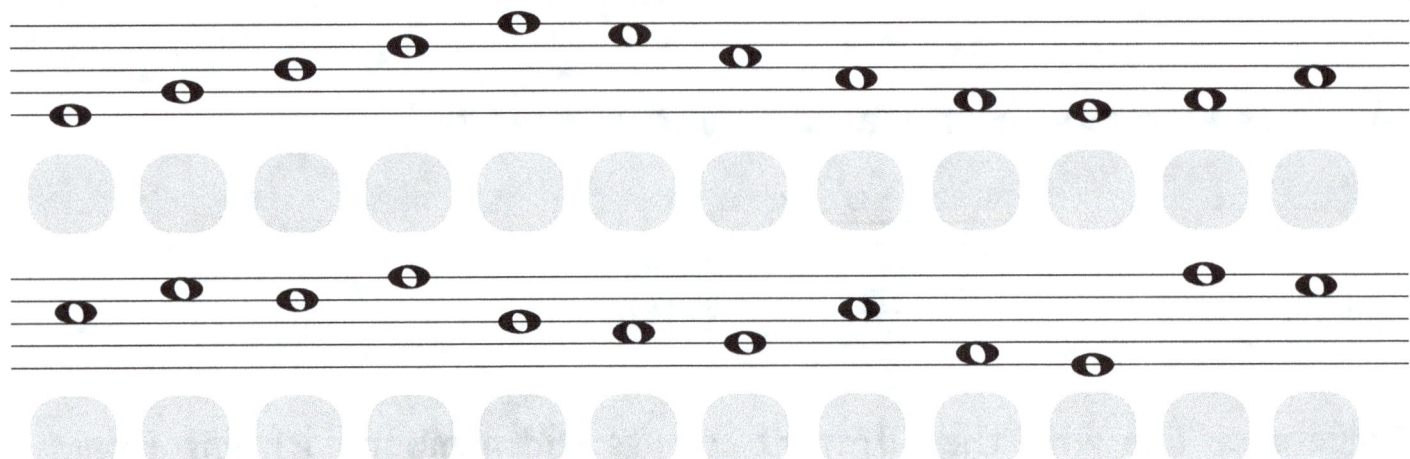

**Help Suzie the Koala find her collection of shells.
Colour the shells accordingly.**

| Shells through the lines red | Shells in the space green |

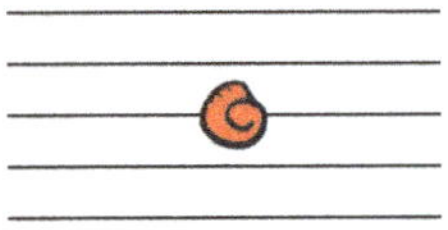

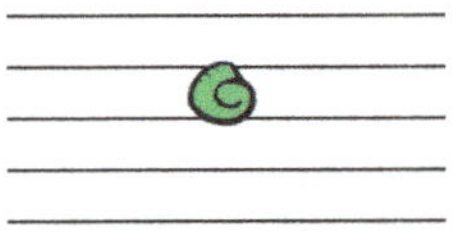

How many shells can you find?

Bass Clef

Music written for the double bass uses the Bass Clef.

A bass clef looks like half of a heart shape. It is used to read low notes. Instruments such as the piano, tuba, trombone, cello and the double bass read from this clef.

Let us practise drawing the bass clefs below around the example before we practise drawing them on the stave.

Now let us trace these bass clefs and then draw 2 more of your own.

(Start on the 4th line where the red dot is.)

The 2 little dots next to the clef goes on the top two spaces 'guarding' the point where we started drawing the clef.

(Start on the 4th line where the red dot is.)

Double Bass Strings

Let's try and remember the names of the open strings.
(Open strings = Name of each string without placing any fingers on it.)

 E   A   D   G

Elephants   Are   Doing   Great

This sentence is called an acronym and helps you remember the names.

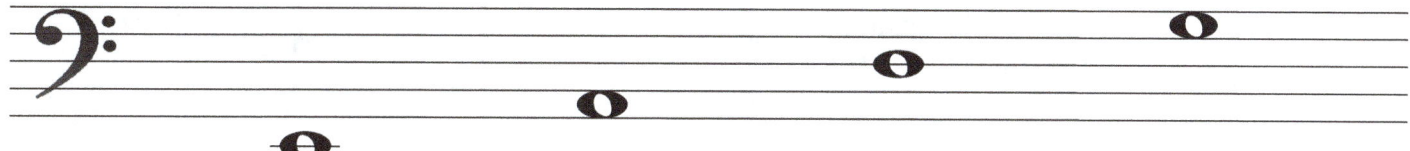

(the extra lines above and below the stave are called ledger/leger lines)

Make up your own acronym.

E_____   A_____   D_____   G_____

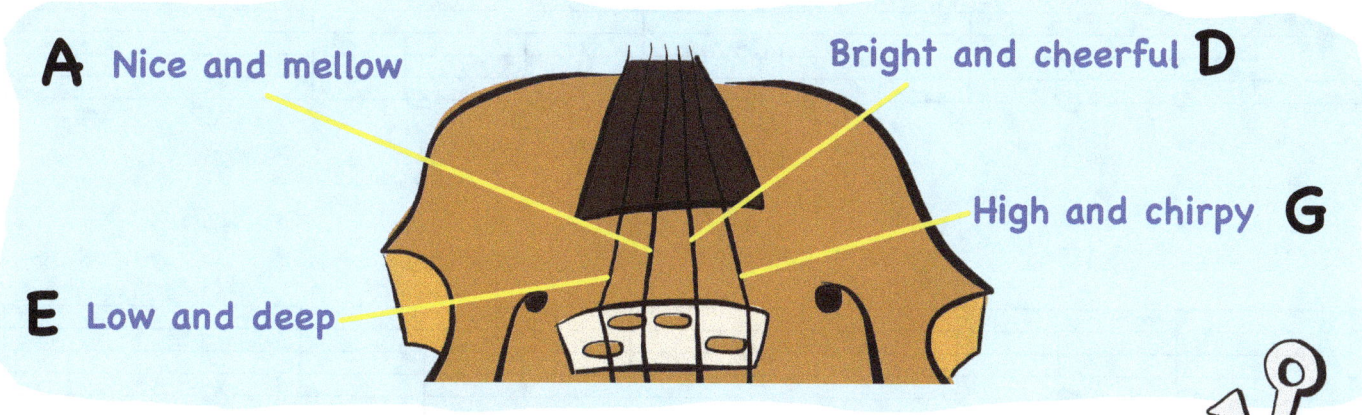

Which string produces the lowest/HEAVIEST sound? _____

Which string produces the highest/lightest sound? _____

Bar Lines

Bars are like classrooms. Each room has a certain amount of students.
Bar lines are like walls of the classrooms. And the double bar line is the end of the building.

Put an arrow where each song would end.

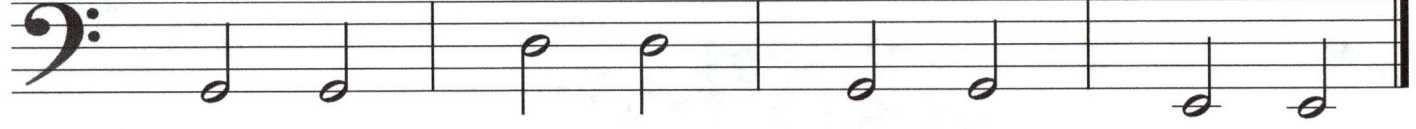

Now try and play each of these short tunes using the bow.

Reading Notes

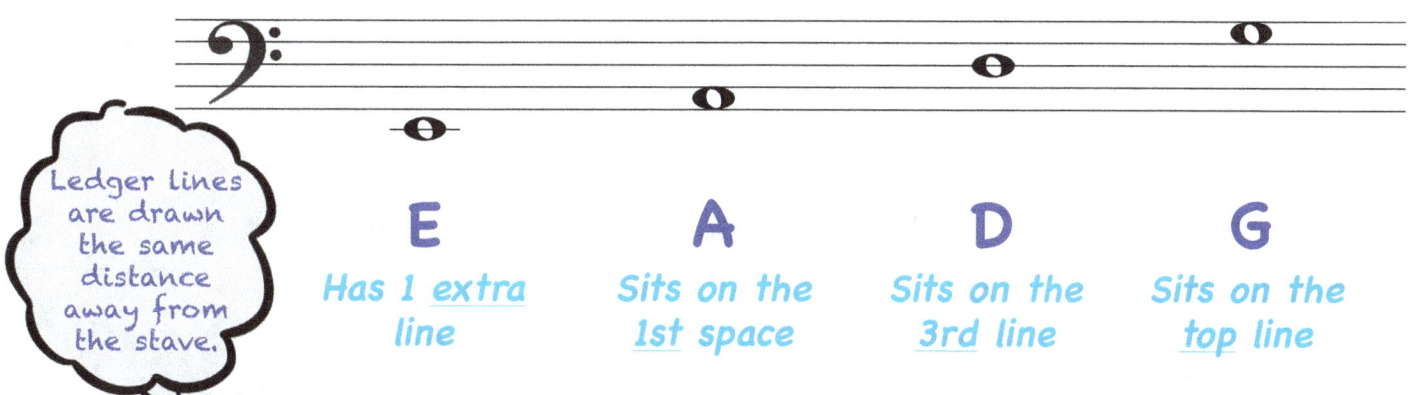

Ledger lines are drawn the same distance away from the stave.

E Has 1 extra line

A Sits on the 1st space

D Sits on the 3rd line

G Sits on the top line

Copy and name the notes of the open strings. (Use capital letters.)

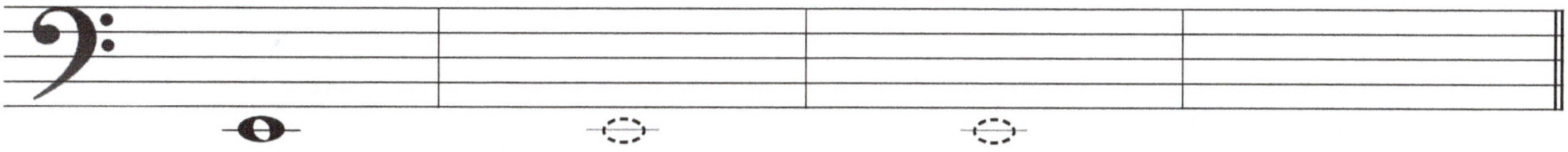

E

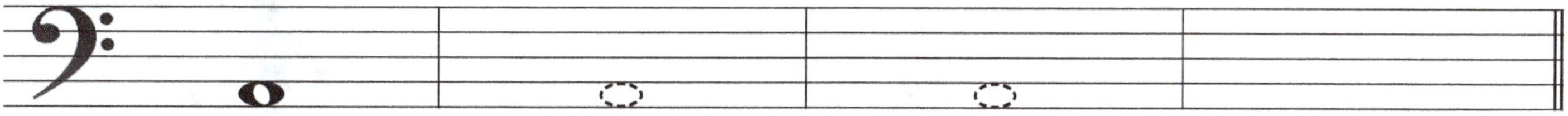

A

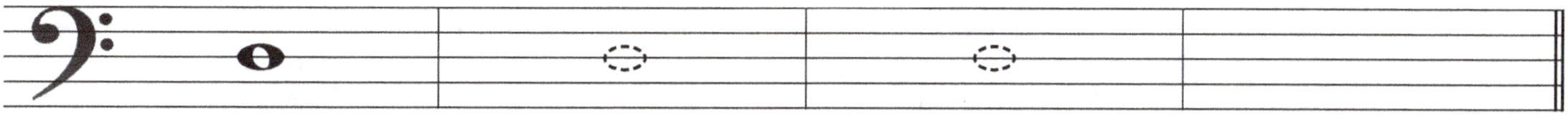

D

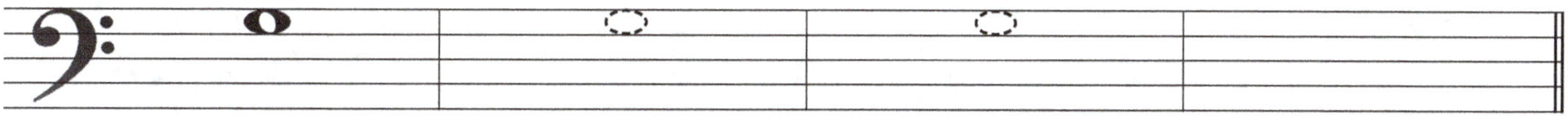

G

Write the letter names of these notes for the open strings.

A

Draw the notes of the open strings.

A   C   G   D   A   D

Match the notes and colour the correct open string.

There are other ways of remembering the names of your notes in between the open string notes.

How many lines does a stave have?

How many spaces does it have?

Below is how we would remember our notes using acronyms.

Gummy   Bear   Dance   Funny   Always

As for the notes in the spaces, all we need to do is use the alphabet which we already know and count up and down between the lines.
Let us see if you can figure out the notes in between.

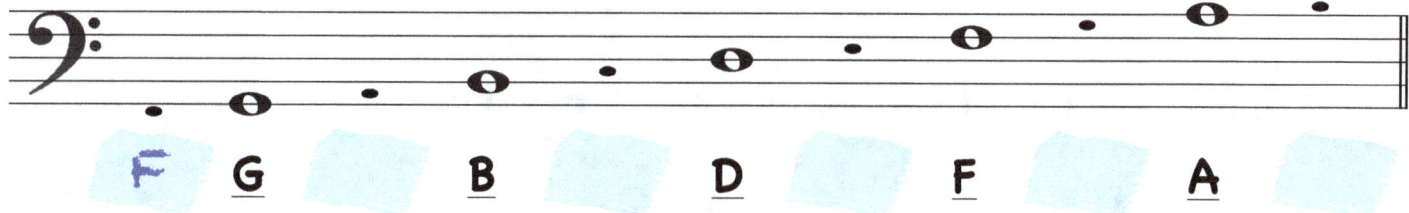

F   G   B   D   F   A

Practise saying the acronyms and see if you would be able to identify the name of the notes.

Do you remember the names of the open strings?

Name these notes.

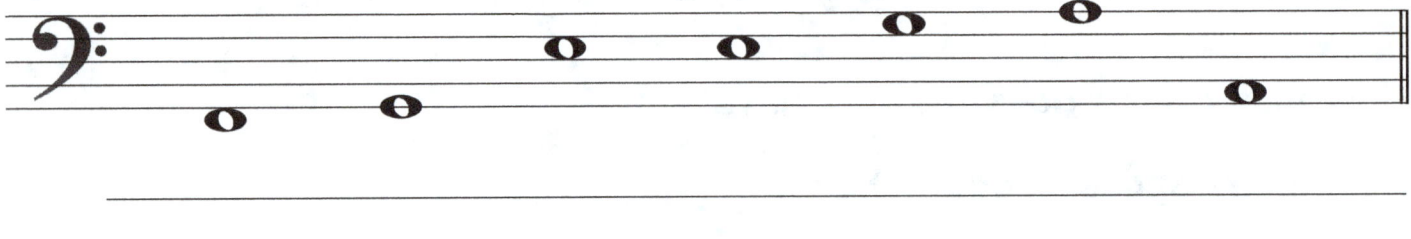

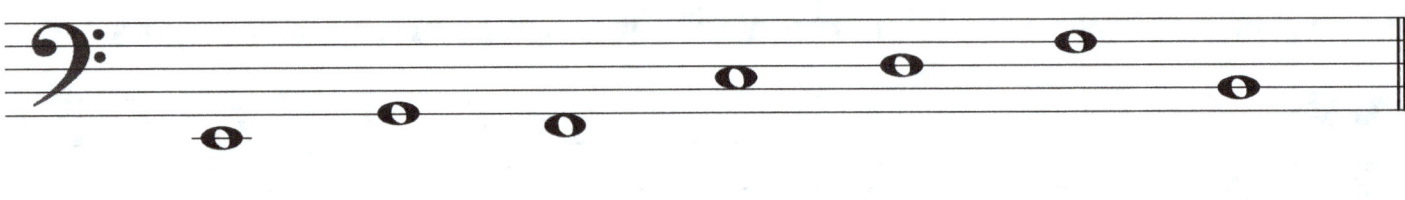

Write your alphabet from A to Z.

_____

_____

For music we only use the letters from A to G.

A   B   C   D   E   F   G

The note after G goes back to A.

See if you can memorize your alphabet backwards from G to A.

By now you should have a few strips or indication markings on your fingerboard.

Finger 1

Finger 2

Finger 3

Finger 4

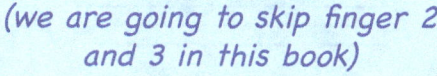

E A D G

(we are going to skip finger 2 and 3 in this book)

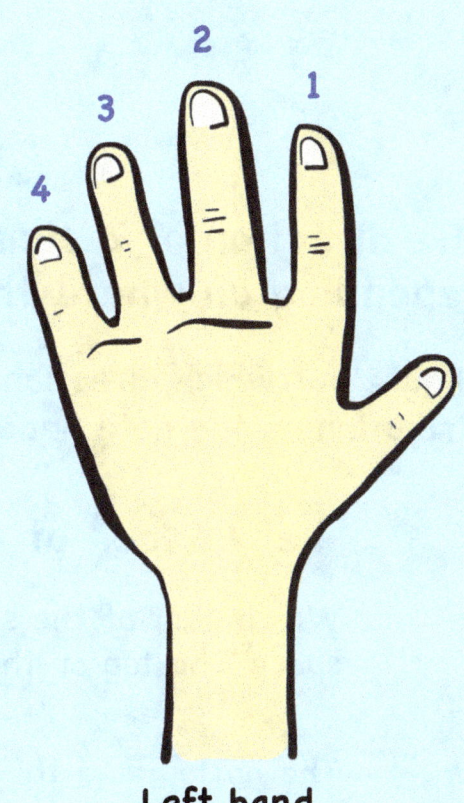

Left hand

Play all the notes of each string using all your fingers starting with the open string.

Call out each finger number while playing each note starting from open string (zero).

Printable <u>flashcards</u> and more <u>work sheet</u> on notes for individual open strings available at **www.stringstastic.com**

Position of Stems

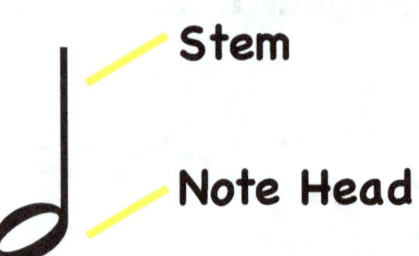

The direction of a stem can be either facing down or up depending on where the note head sits on the stave.

To figure out which direction the stem would face, think of the space distribution of the note heads and stems making them even on the stave.

Let us look at the notes on the middle line.

Which part of the stave has more space. The top or the bottom?

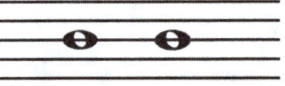

The bottom and the top part of the stave has the same amount of space.

Because of this, the stems can face either upwards or downwards.

Let us look at the notes from the middle line downwards.
(Low notes)

Which part of the stave has more space. The top or the bottom?

The top part of the stave has more space.

Because of this, the stems will face upwards.
Remember that the stems are drawn on the right side of the note to make the note look like the letter 'd'.

Let us look at the notes from the middle line upwards.
(High notes)

Which part of the stave has more space. The top or the bottom?

The bottom part of the stave has more space.

Because of this, the stems will face downwards.
Remember that the stems are drawn on the left side of the note to make the note look like a letter 'P'.

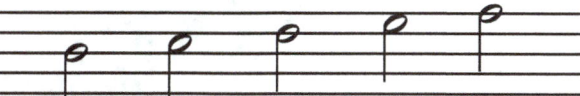

The note head is like a seed and the stem is the stick growing out. The direction of a stem can be either facing down or up depending on which part of the stave has more space.

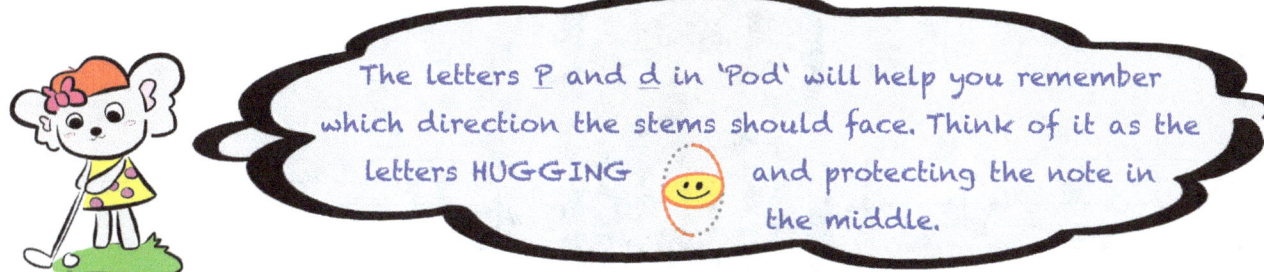

The letters P and d in 'Pod' will help you remember which direction the stems should face. Think of it as the letters HUGGING and protecting the note in the middle.

Add a stem to every note.

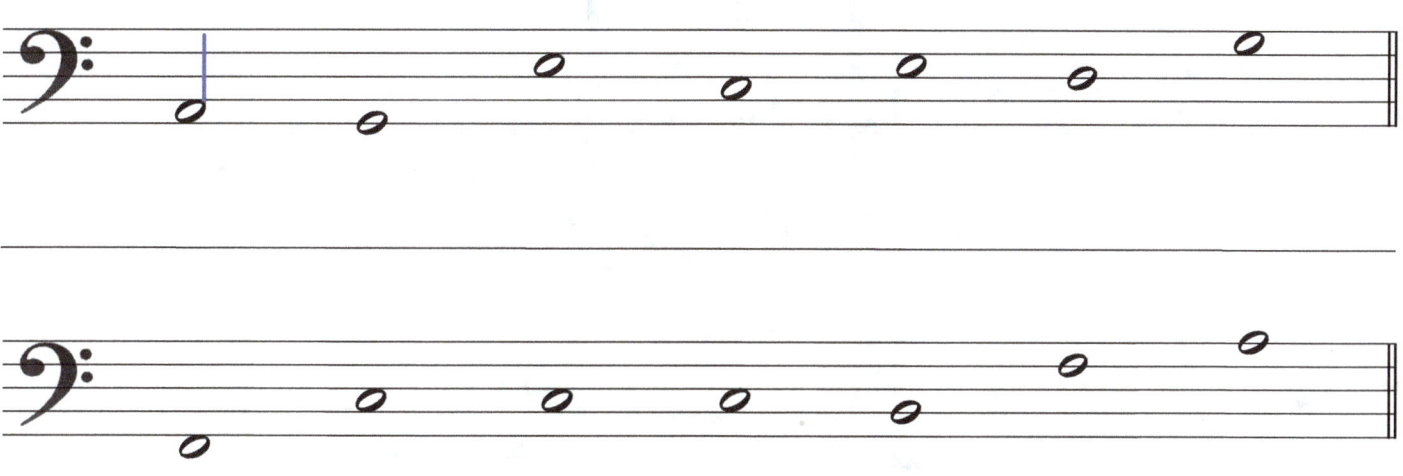

Now let us name the notes above.

Some stems are facing the wrong direction. Correct them so they sit properly on the stave.

Tip: "Replant" the seeds and figure out which direction they would grow.

Note Values

NOTE	NOTE VALUE	NAME
♩	1	Crotchet
♪ (half note)	2	Minim
♩. (dotted half)	3	Dotted minim
𝅝	4	Semibreve

Draw the notes and their value in each bar.

Crotchet

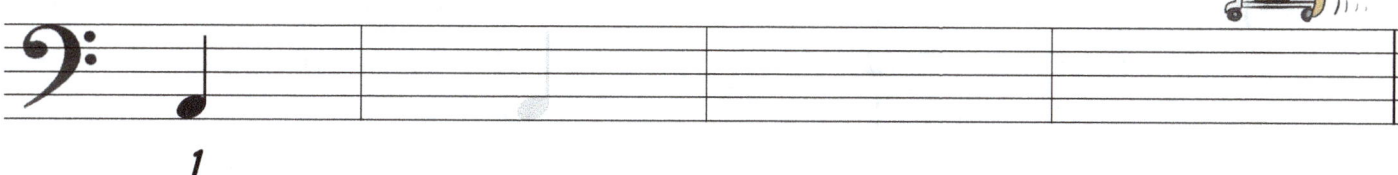

1

Minim

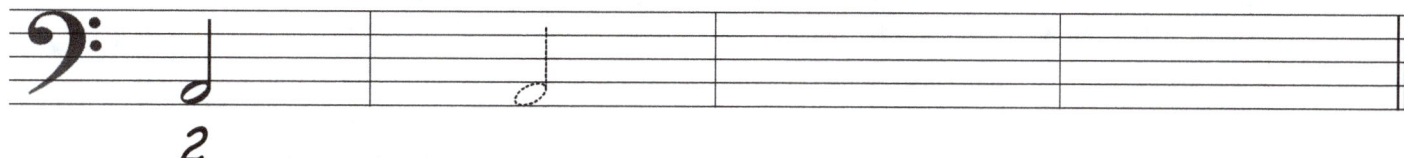

2

Dotted Minim

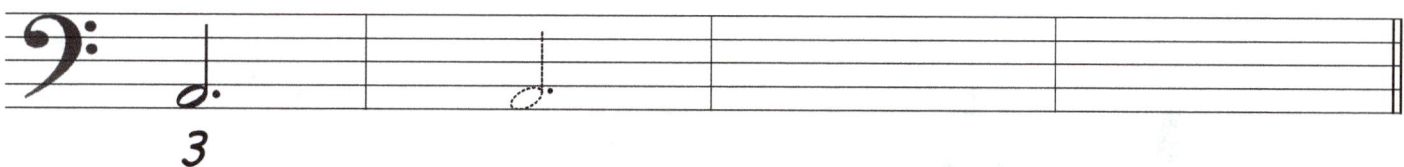

3

Semibreve

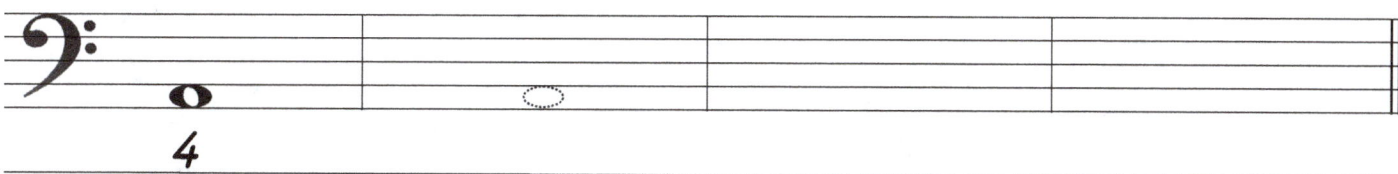

4

Write the note value of each note.

Match the notes to the correct name.

NOTES	NAMES
o	Minim
d.	Semibreve
d	Dotted minim
♩	Crotchet

Count the number in each group. Draw the total value of each group. (Use crotchet note values.)

(You can draw more than one note if the value is more than 4 counts.)

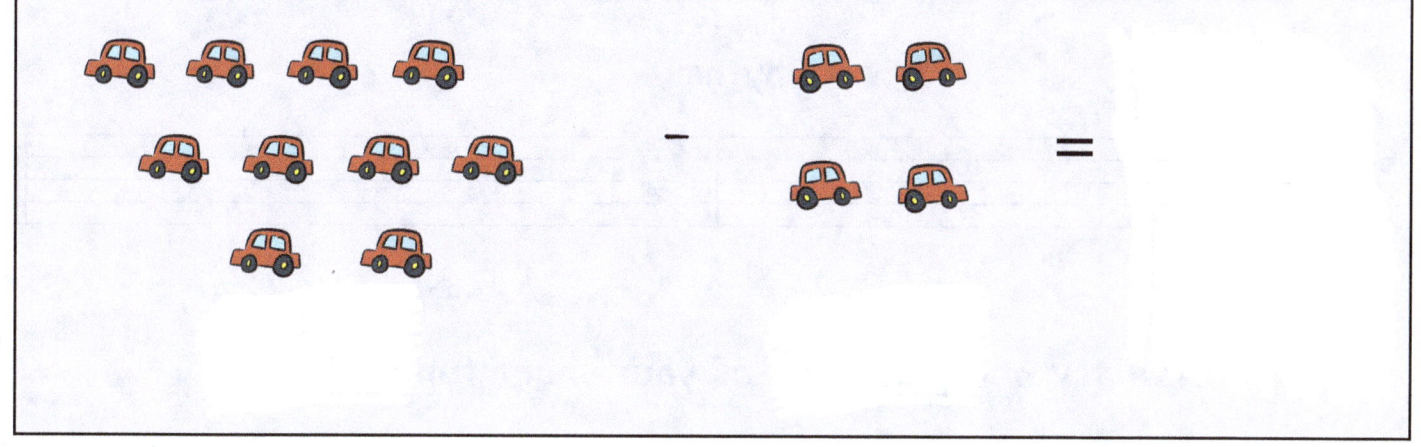

Clap and count the beats.

Using the rhythms above, write your own music using the open string notes (E, A, D, G). You can write TWO different tunes on the same rhythm.

Example:

Rhythm 1

Rhythm 2

Rhythm 3

Rhythm 4

Now try and play each of your short tunes pizz.

What have we learnt so far?

1. How many strings does a double bass have? Name them.

   _____

2. Label and name the different parts of the double bass using the words given.

| bridge |
| end pin |
| bow |
| f holes |
| tail piece |
| fingerboard |
| frog |
| horse hair |
| pegs |
| scroll |

3. Fill in the blanks.

SYMBOL	NAME
𝄢	
	stave
(staff lines)	
♩ (quarter note with arrow)	

SYMBOL	NAME	COUNT
	semibreve	
♩		
𝅗𝅥		
		3

4. Mark the correct string on the double bass.

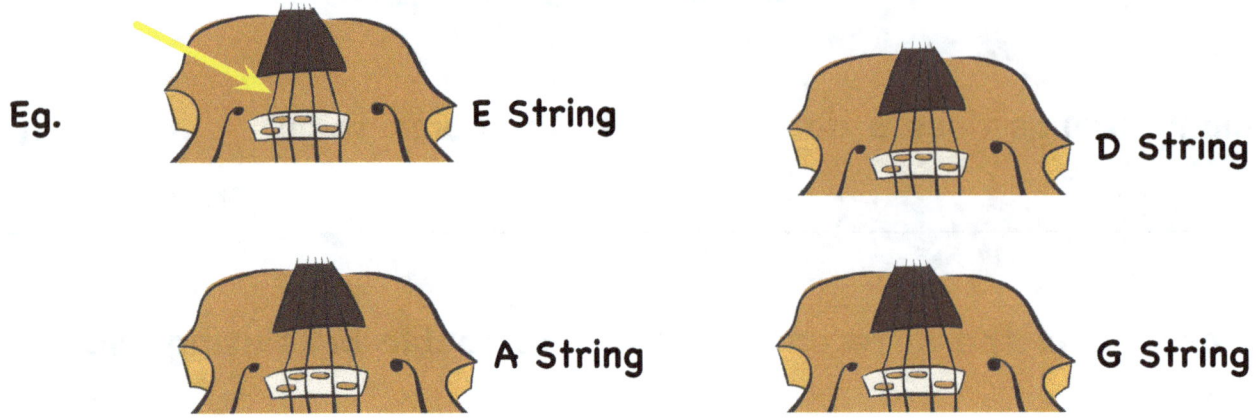

5. Draw and name these notes on the open string in semibreves.

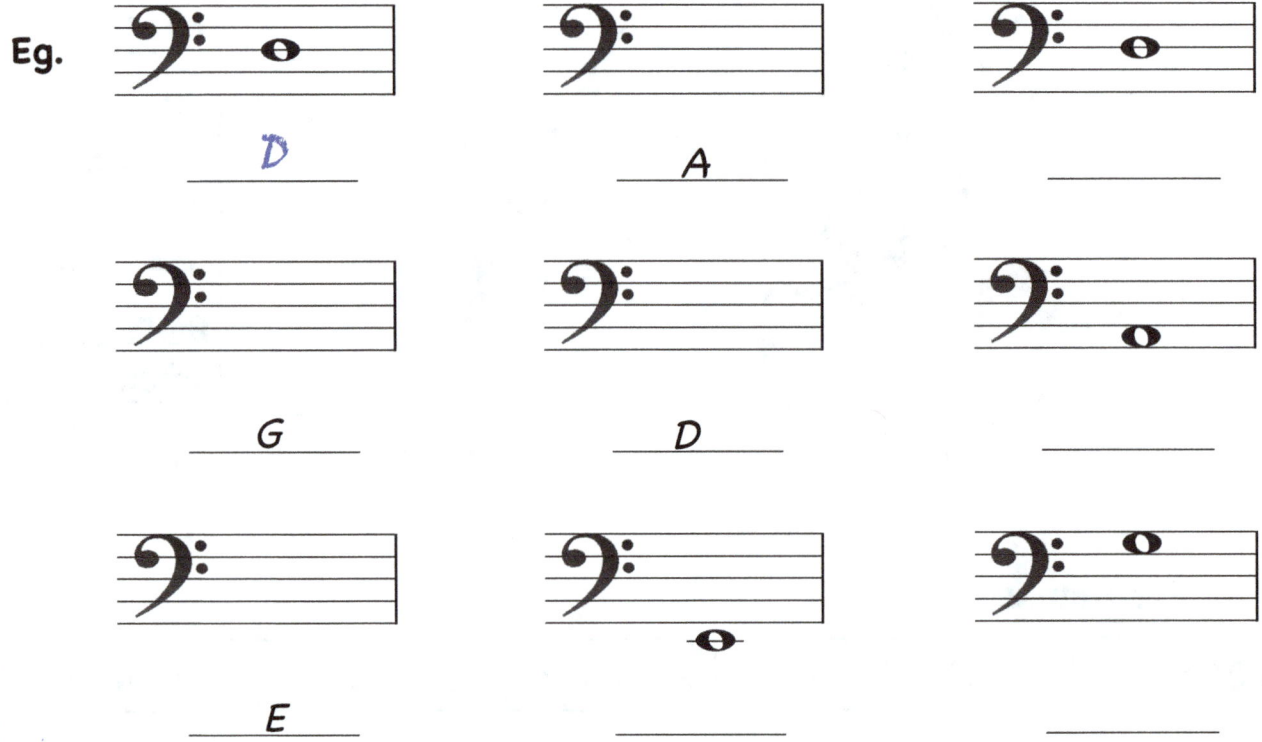

6. What letter note comes after G in music?

Rests

NOTE	REST		NOTE VALUE
♩	𝄽	If you straighten this wavy line, it looks like the number 1	1
𝅗𝅥	▬	Hat closed half full	2
𝅝	▬	You can fill more things with the hat open	4

▬ may also be used as a whole bar rest.

Copy each rest and count them in each bar.

Crotchet rest (lightning/slanted ≳ + capital C)

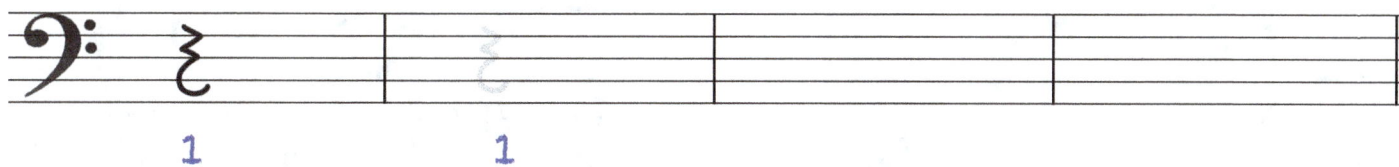

1   1

Minim rest (sitting on 3rd line)

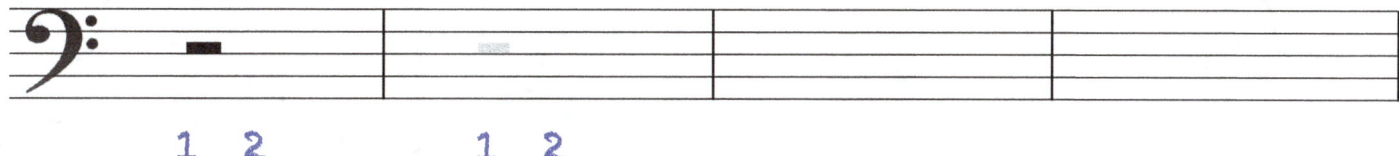

1 2   1 2

Semibreve rest (hanging on 4th line)

1 2 3 4   1 2 3 4

Write down the value of each rest.

The sea creatures in Atlantic City live in their own luxurious underwater apartment. Help them find their correct place.

Time Signature

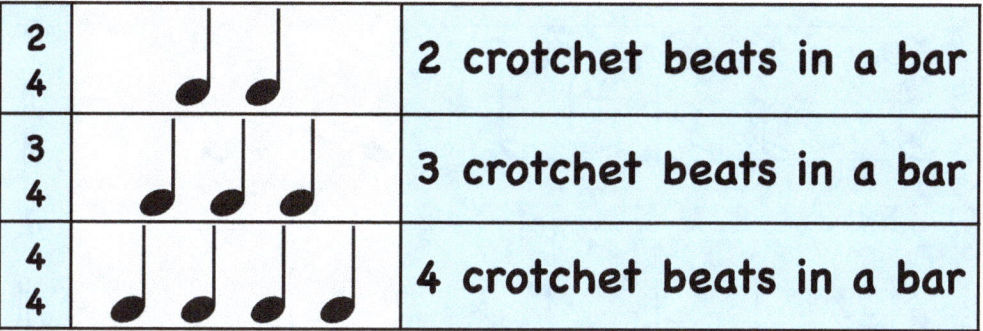

Information: 3 → top number means the number of beats in a measure.

Write in the beats of each bar.

Write in the correct beats and time signature.

Put in the bar lines and write in the beats.

Write in the beats for each of these bars.

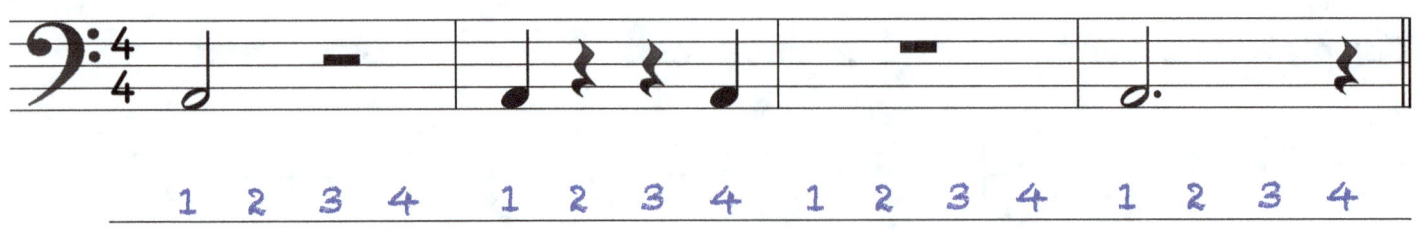

1 2 3 4   1 2 3 4   1 2 3 4   1 2 3 4

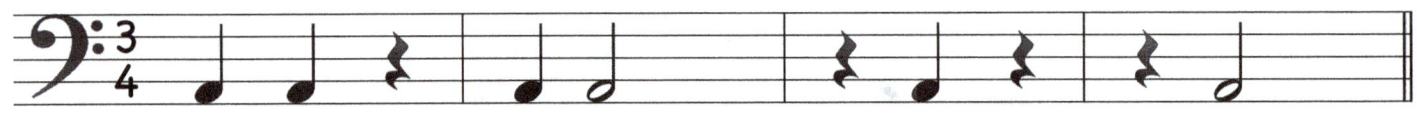

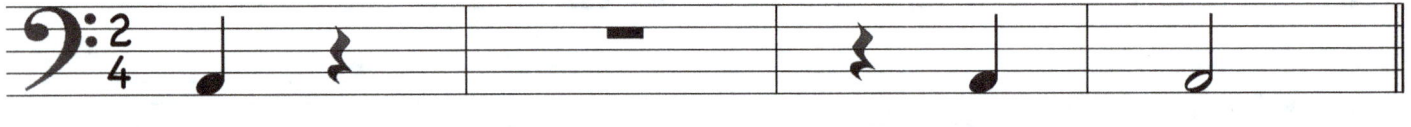

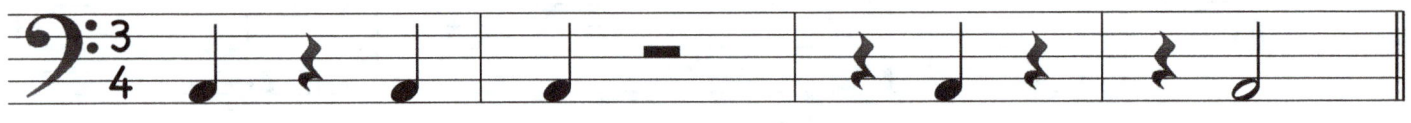

Accidentals

♭	♮	♯
Flat (Lower)	Natural (Normal = no change)	Sharp (Higher)

♯ **Sharp** ↑ = raises a note by 1 step
(raises the finger by 1 step)

♭ **Flat** ↓ = lowers a note by 1 step
(lowers the finger by 1 step)

♮ **Natural** = puts a note back to its original pitch

In order, arrange the accidental from highest to lowest and name the accidentals.

ACCIDENTALS	NAME
♯	

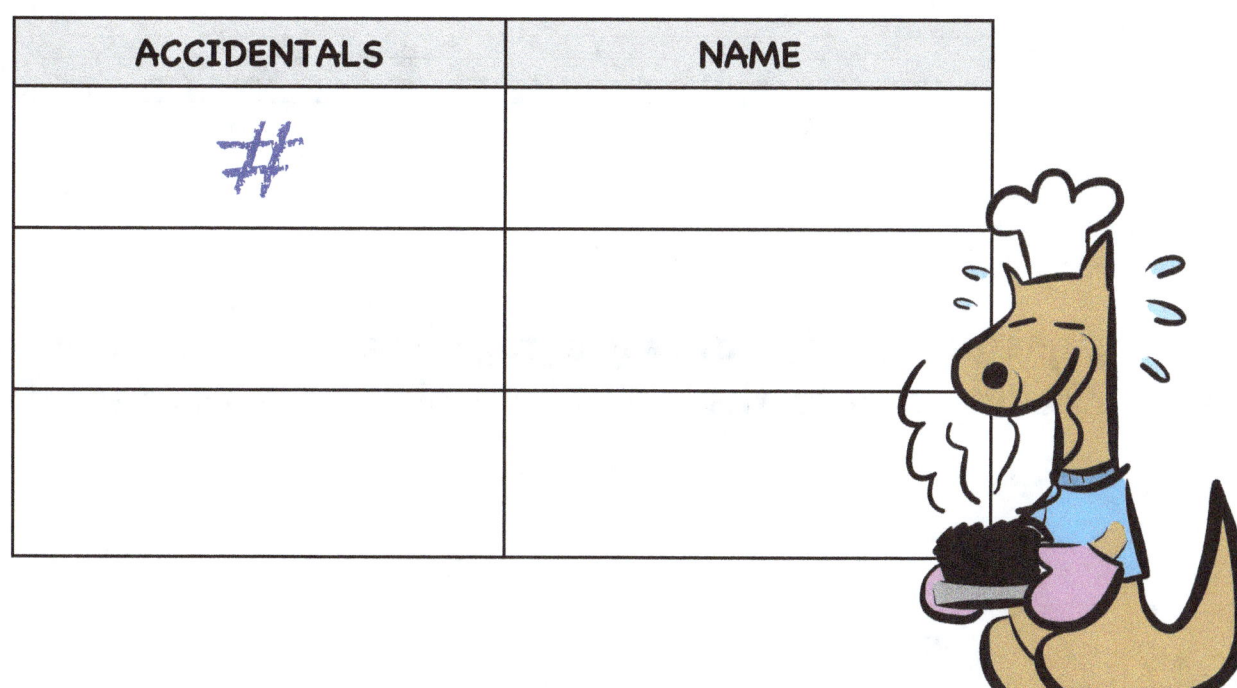

The sharp sign should be drawn on the same space or line as the note head.

Trace the sharp signs below and draw THREE more through any line and THREE more in any space.

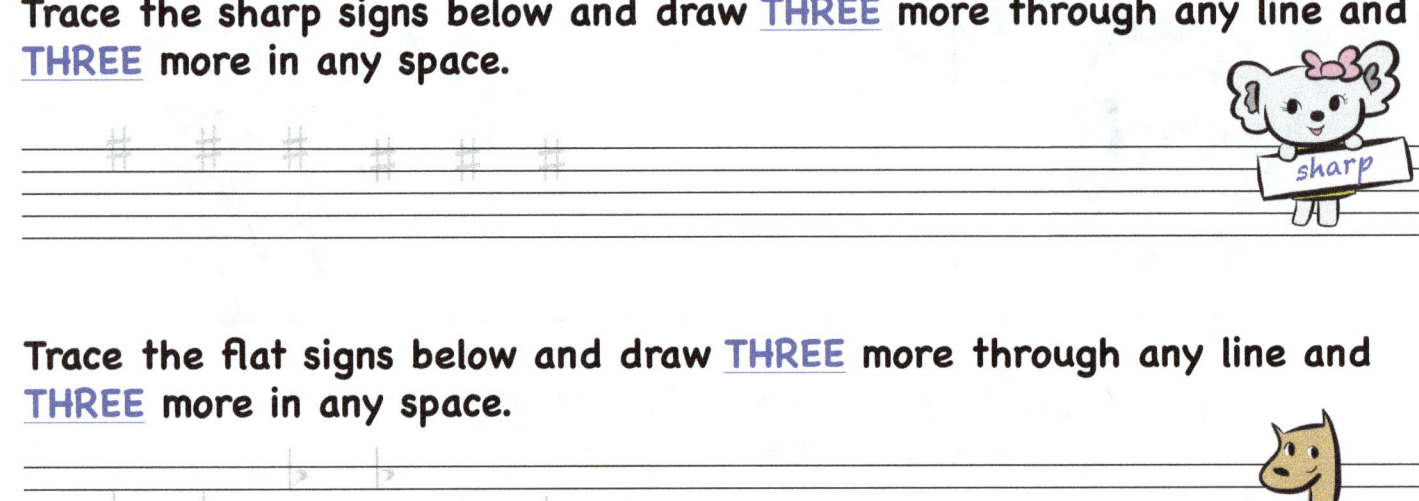

Trace the flat signs below and draw THREE more through any line and THREE more in any space.

Trace the natural signs below and draw THREE more through any line and THREE more in any space.

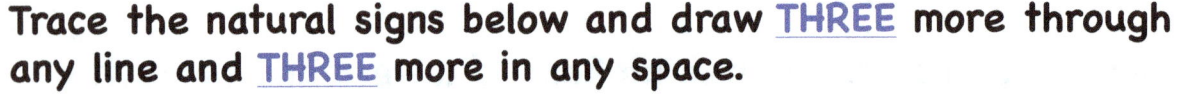

These signs are always drawn <u>before</u> the note head. However, when labelling a note the accidental signs are written <u>after</u> the note.

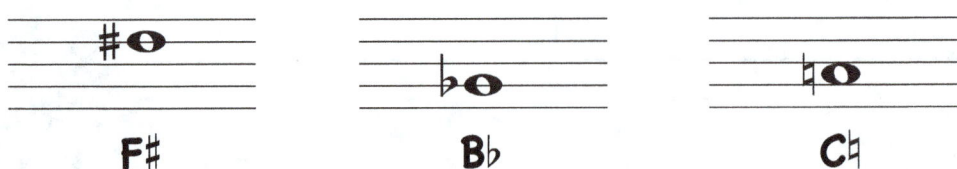

Put a sharp (#) before every note.

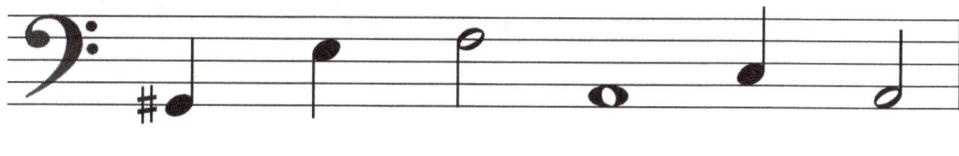

Put a flat (♭) before every note.

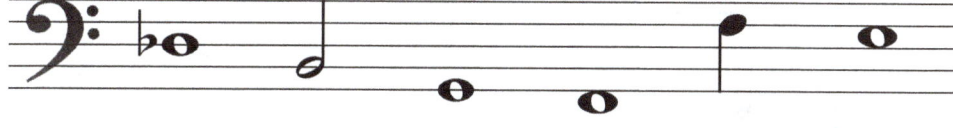

Now name the notes above.

Name the notes below.

D String

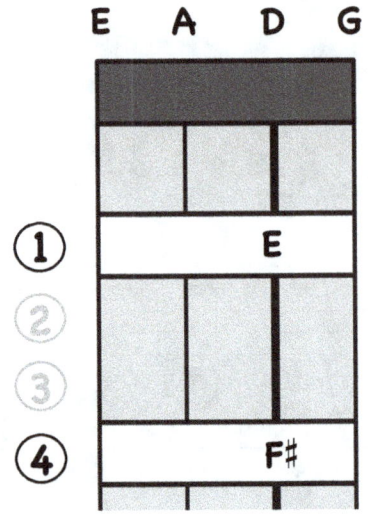
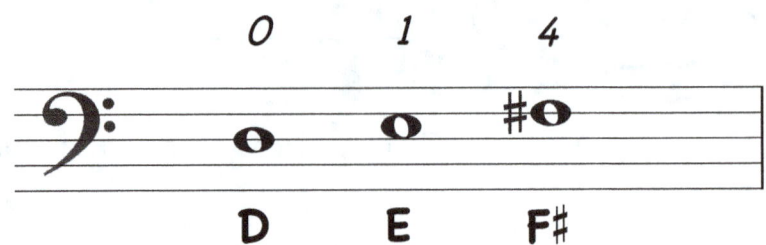

(we are going to skip finger 2 and 3)

Copy each note below and their fingering accordingly.

Name the notes and their fingering accordingly.

   F#

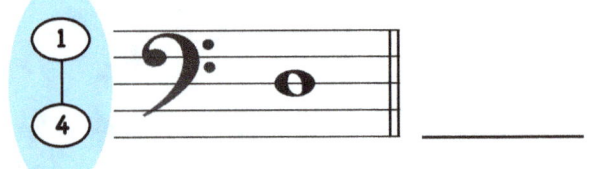

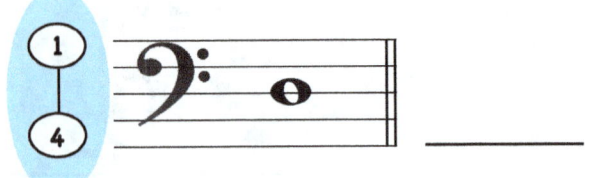

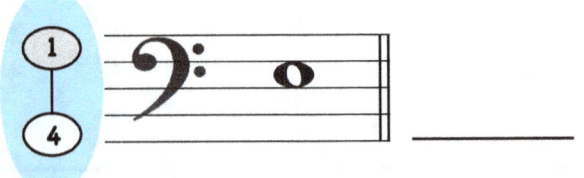

Two children went to the pet shop. Each tries to touch the animals with their finger. Colour the animals according to the finger they used.

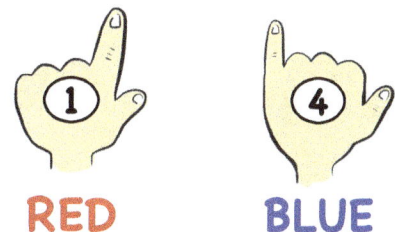

RED   BLUE

PET SHOP

Strings and Note Names

Remember the letters you use in music to name the music notes? What are they? _____

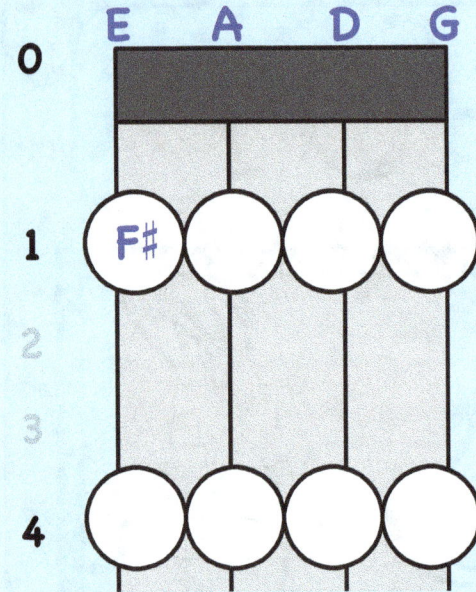

Name each fingering of the main lines on the double bass according to your music alphabet.

(Finger 0, 1, 4)

The open strings are already given.

Now, add a SHARP sign (#) on the 4th finger on all the strings except on the G string.

NOTE: Only finger 1 tab on the E string has a # which has already been done for you.

Which finger tab has no sharps?

Tip: When playing the 4th finger, ALL fingers are standing, pressing on the string EXCEPT the 1st finger.

Pluck each note on your double bass while saying the letter names of each note starting on the open E string.

Now try playing and naming each note backwards starting on finger 4 on the G string.

A String

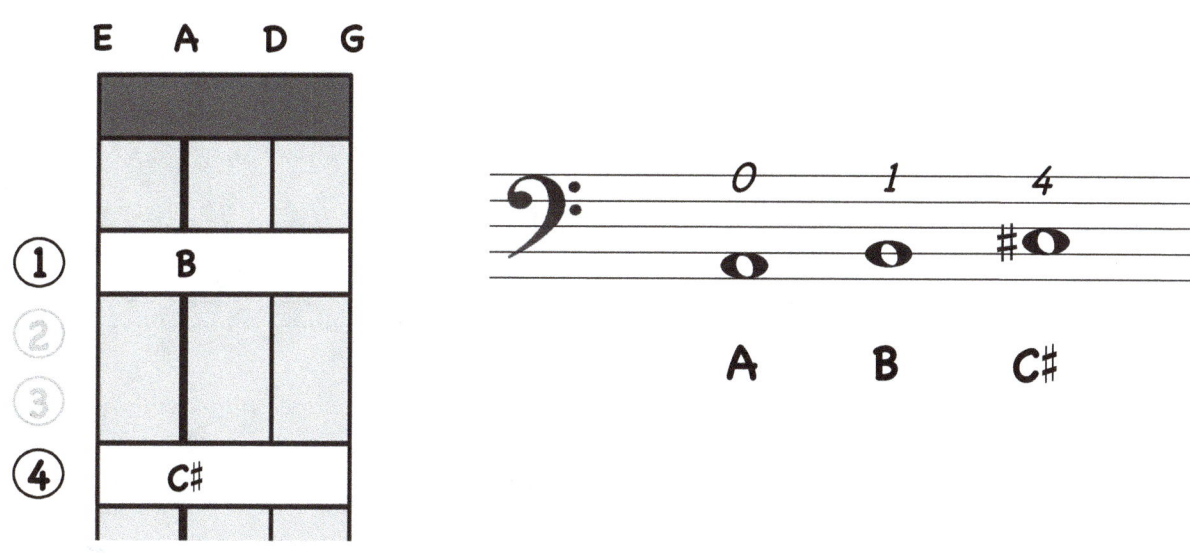

Copy each note below and their fingering accordingly.

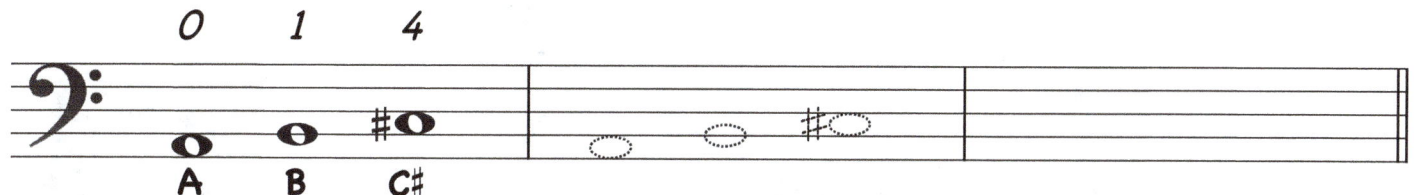

Fill in the blanks.

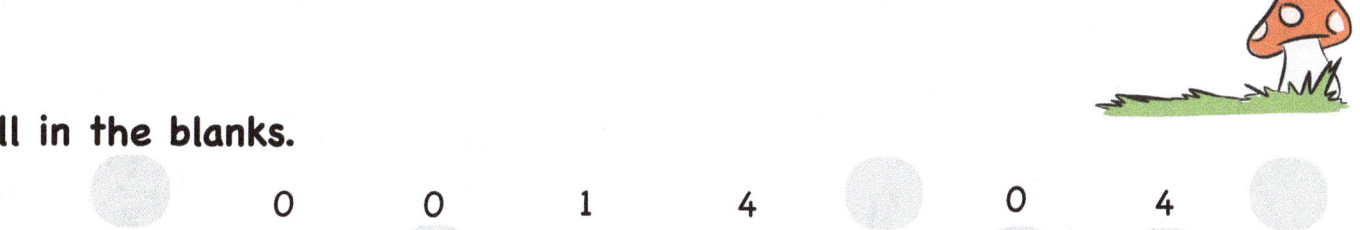

Using minim notes, draw the notes of these fingering on the A string and name the notes.

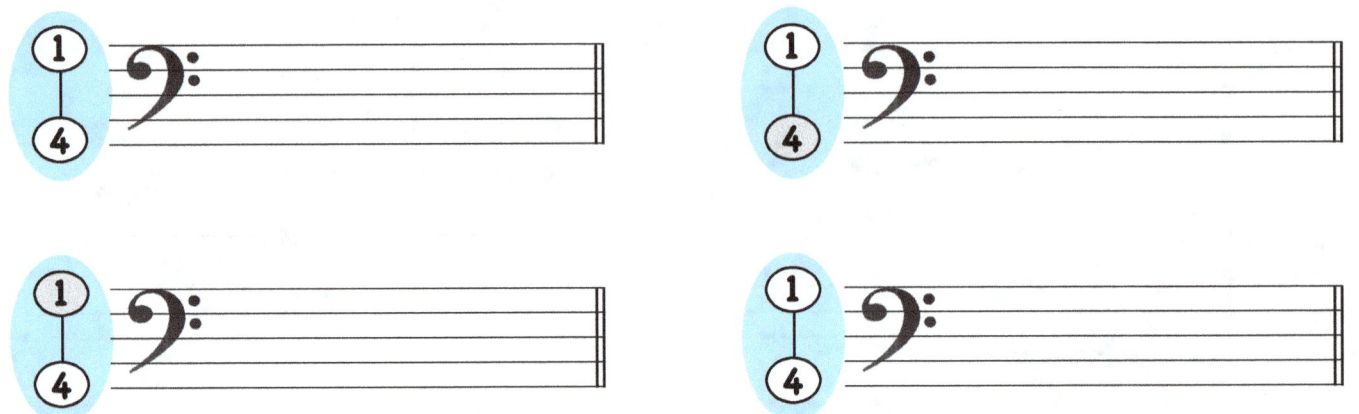

Tommy and his friends all finish their music lessons at the same time. Who reaches home 1st?

Pete the Pig:

Max the Turtle:

Tommy the Kangaroo:

Kate the Penguin:

Revision D and A Strings

In semibreves, draw the notes as shown, including the open string notes.

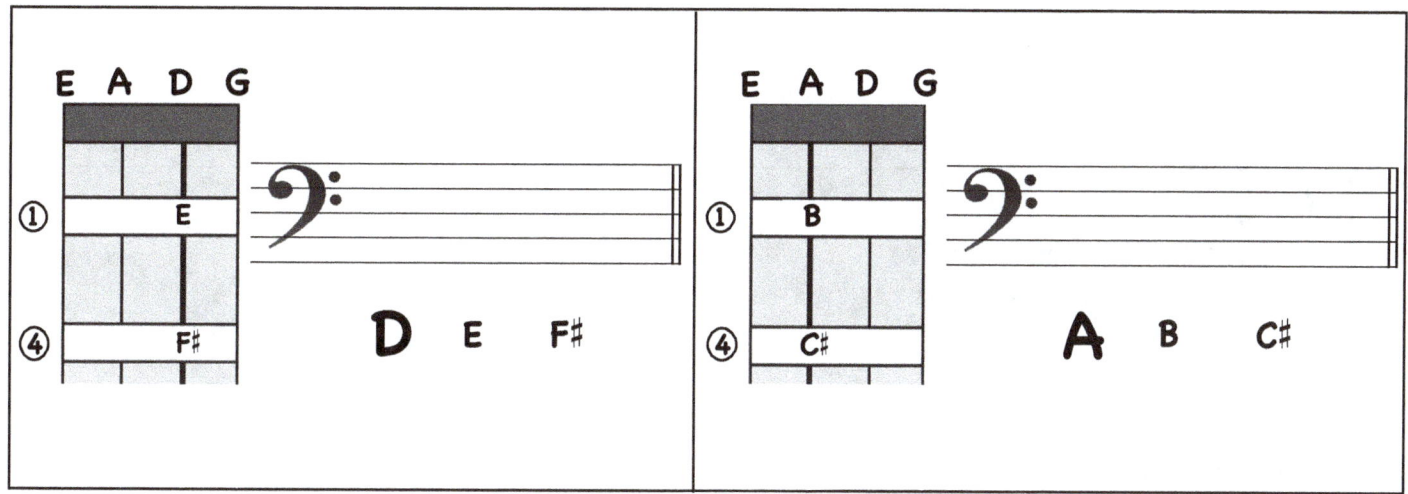

Which fingering do you use on these notes?

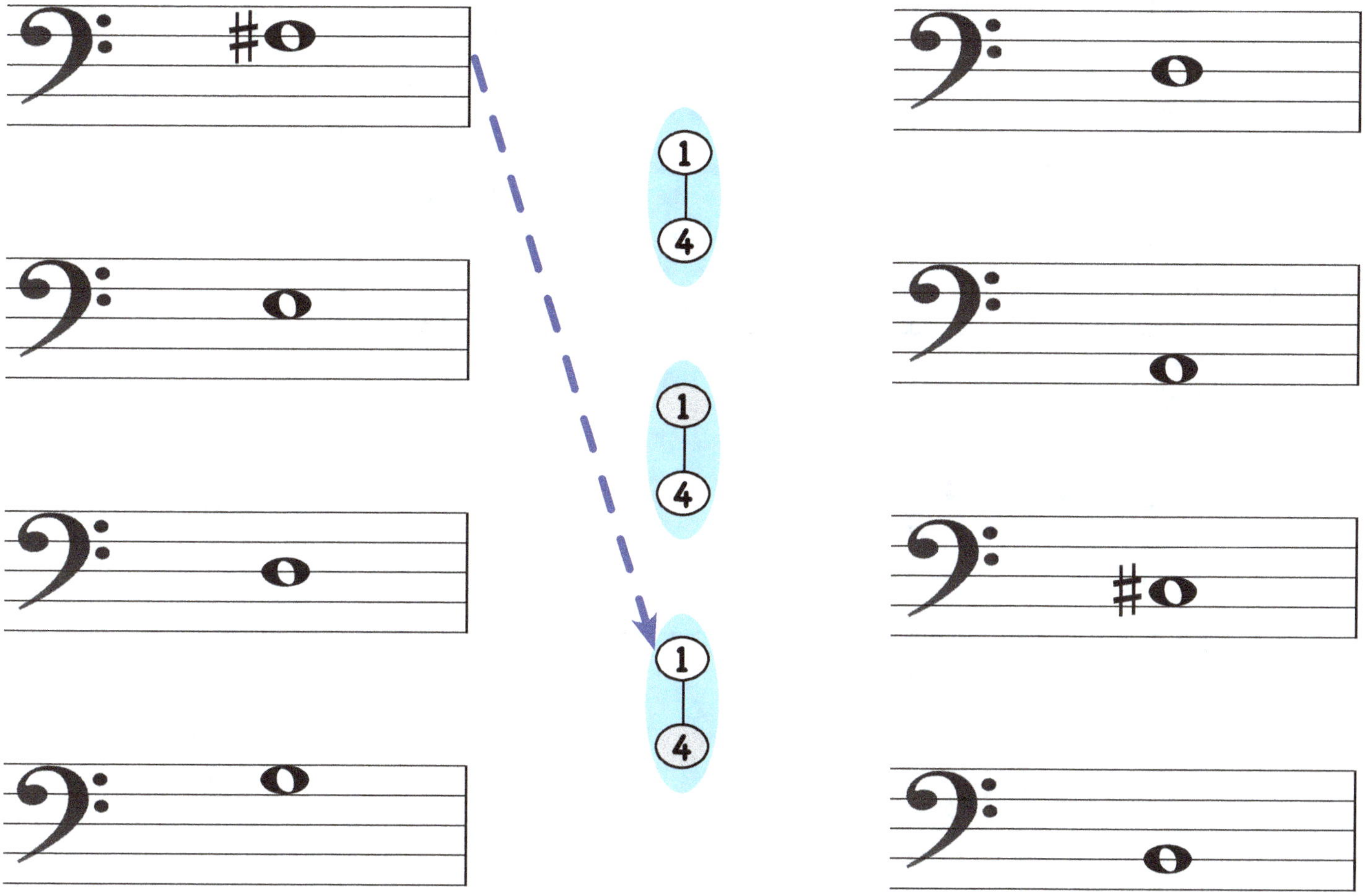

Name each note according to the fingering and label it on the string.

STRINGS	FINGERING	NAME OF THE NOTE
D string	0	D
D string		F#
A string	1	
D string	4	
D string		E
A string		A

G String

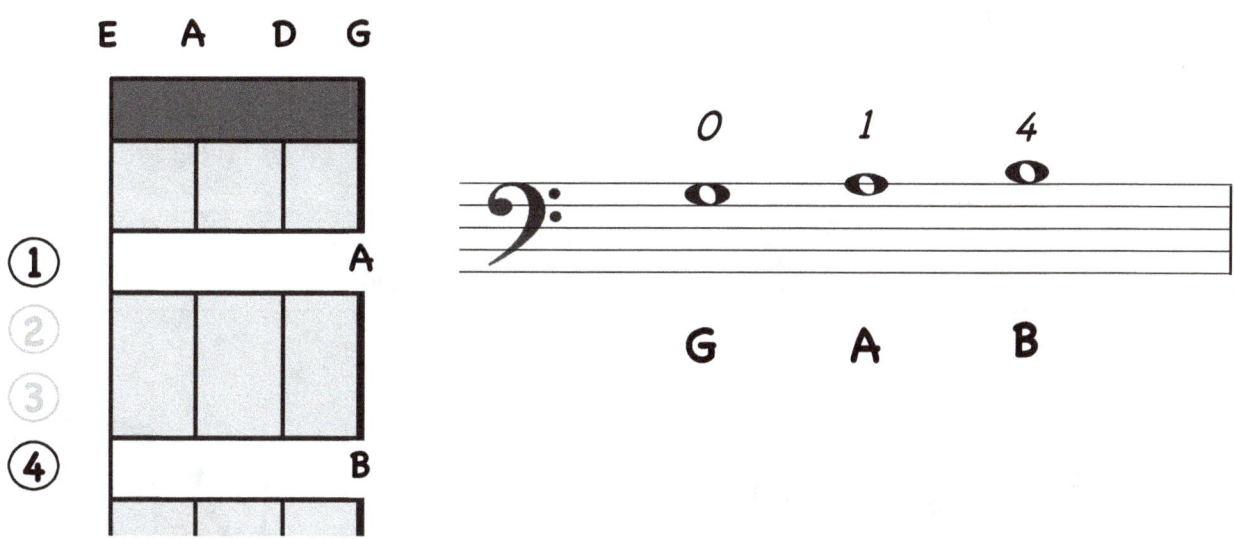

Copy each note below and their fingering accordingly.

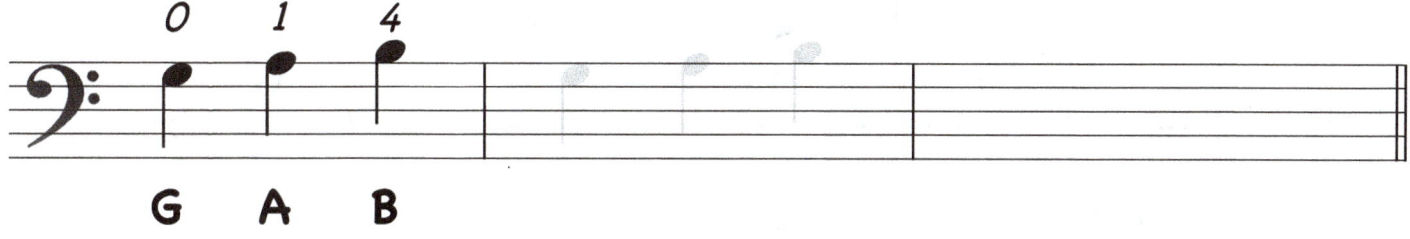

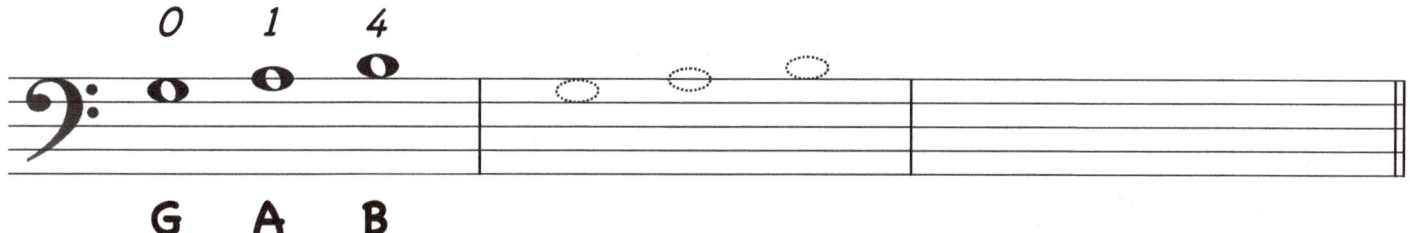

Using semibreves, draw the notes of these fingerings and name the notes on the G string.

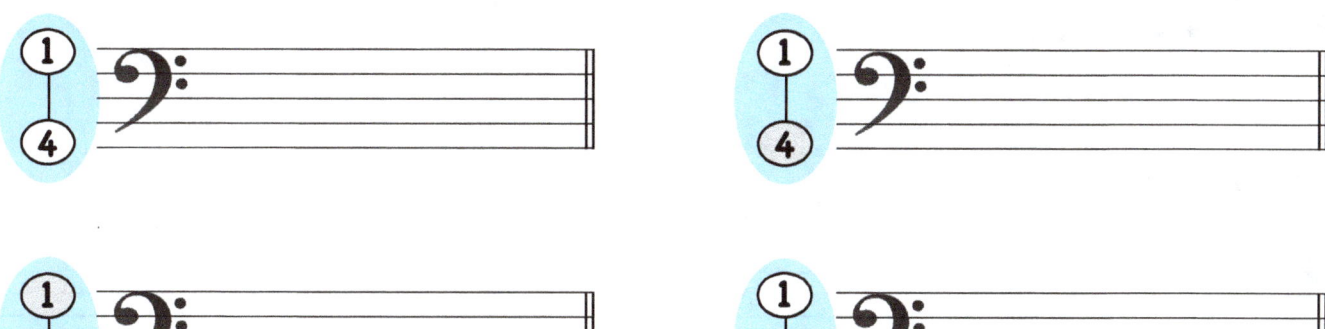

46

Which fingers are used to play these notes?

Colour the fingering and name the note.

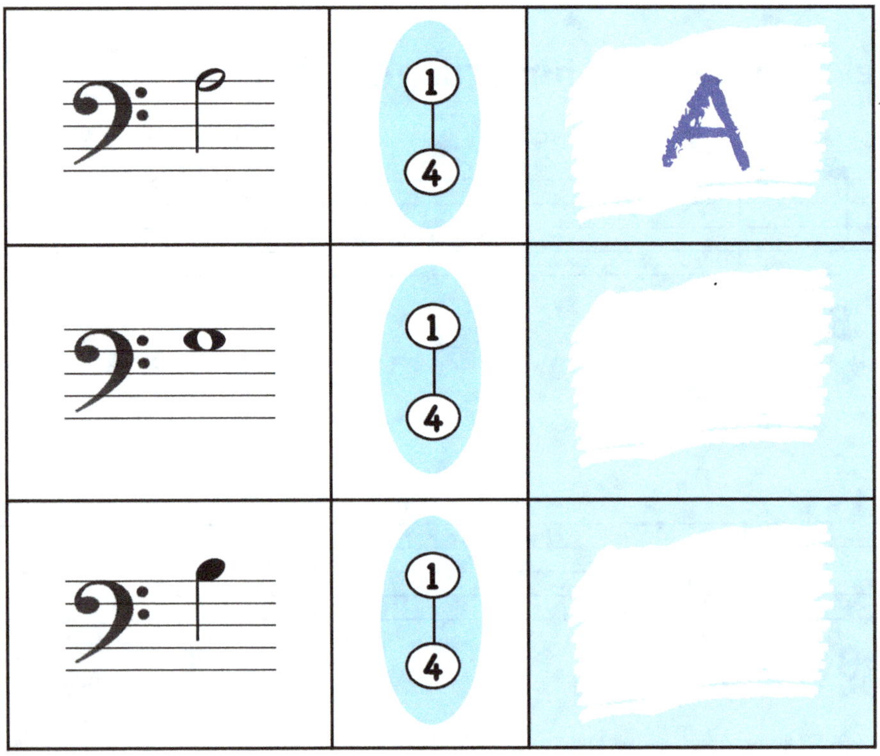

𝄢 ♩	① — ④	A
𝄢 𝅝	① — ④	
𝄢 ♩	① — ④	

Name the notes.

G

E String

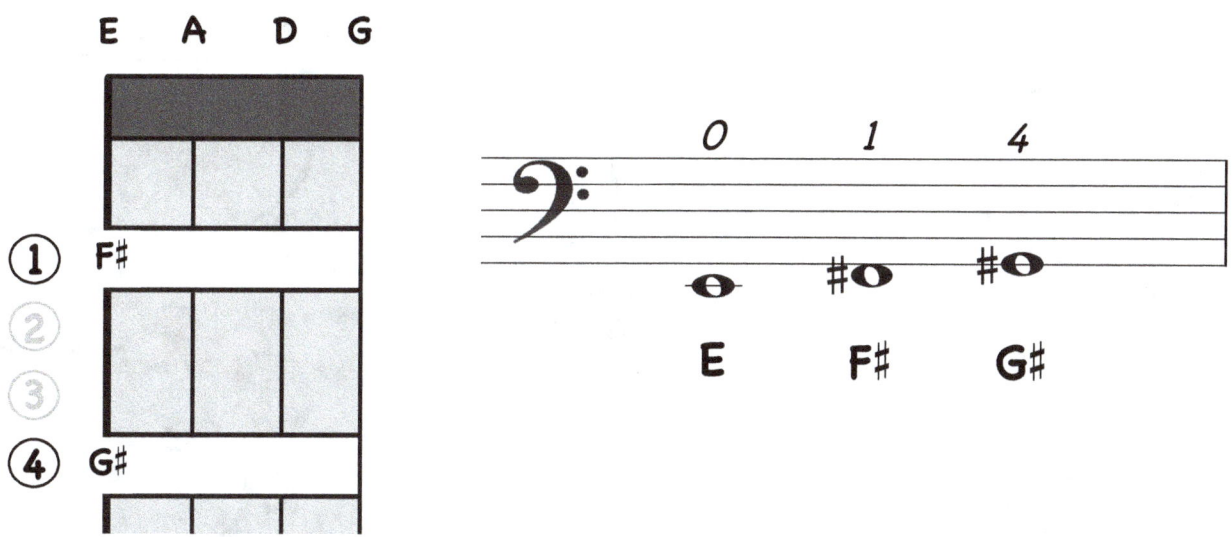

Copy each note below and their fingering accordingly.

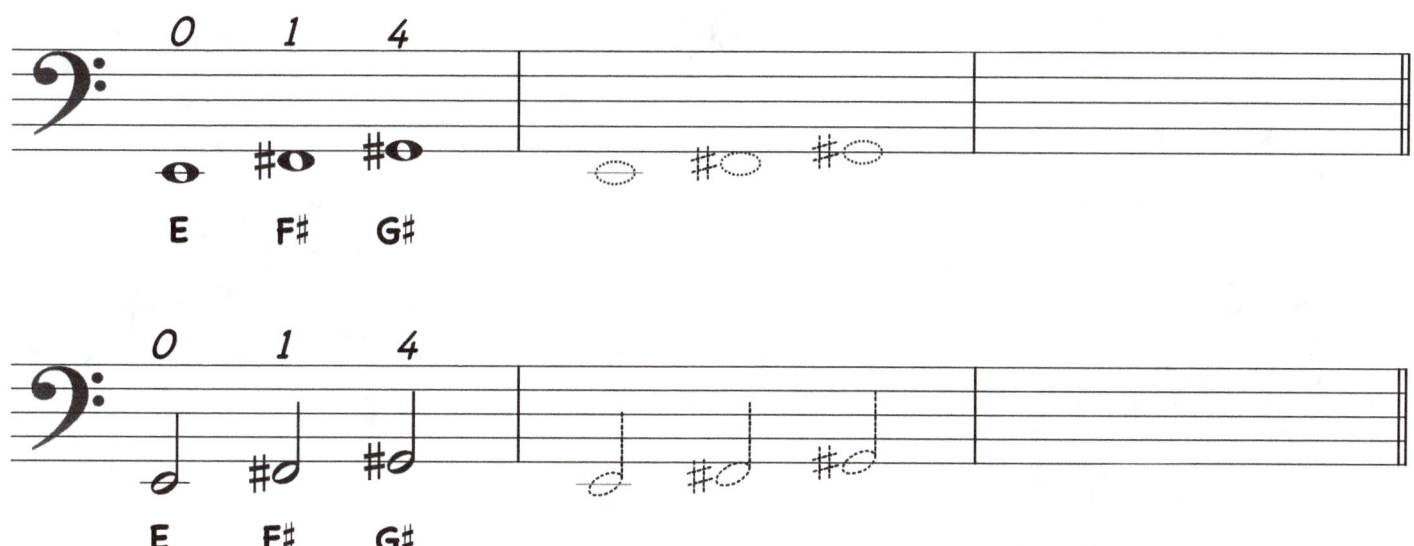

Now play these notes on the double bass while naming them aloud.

Name the notes and its fingering.

48

Match the fingering on these notes.

Revision (on all strings)

1. Draw all the open string notes according to the name given.

E   A   D   G

2. Name the string where each of these notes are found.

[fingering]	G	E String	[fingering]	A	
[fingering]	E		[fingering]	F♯	
[fingering]	B		[fingering]	E	
[fingering]	C♯		[fingering]	D	
[fingering]	A		[fingering]	F♯	

3. Write down the fingering and name the notes.

4

G♯

4. Using semibreve notes, draw these notes on the stave.

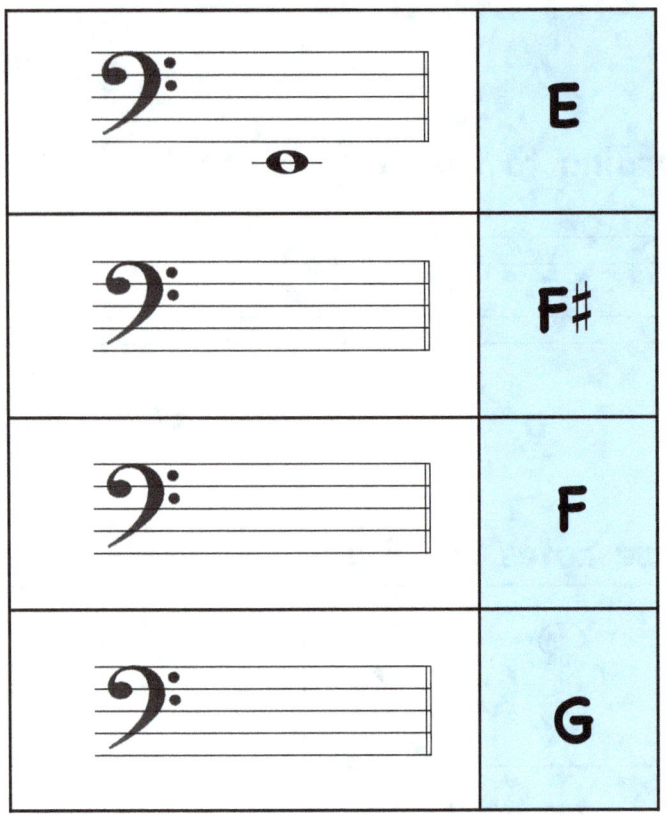
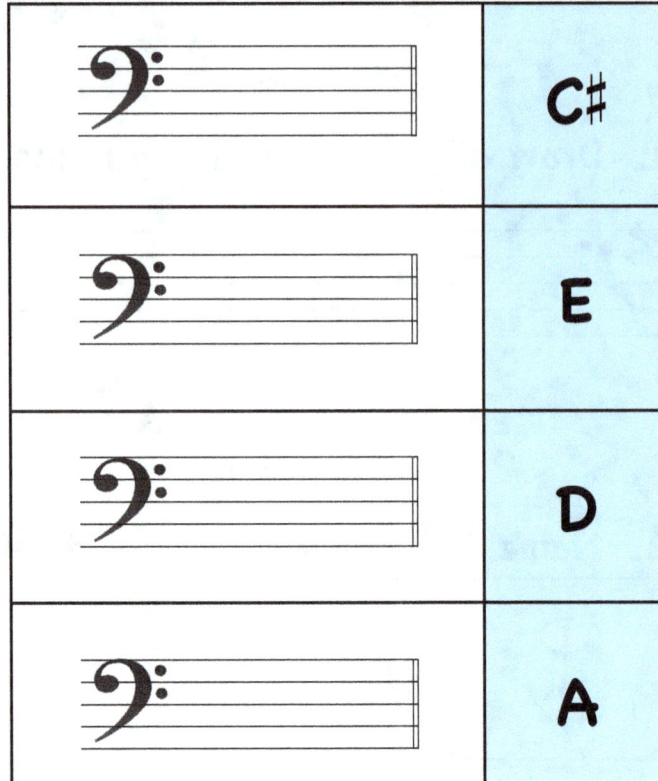

5. Using any note values to draw 2 different notes and colour in their fingering.

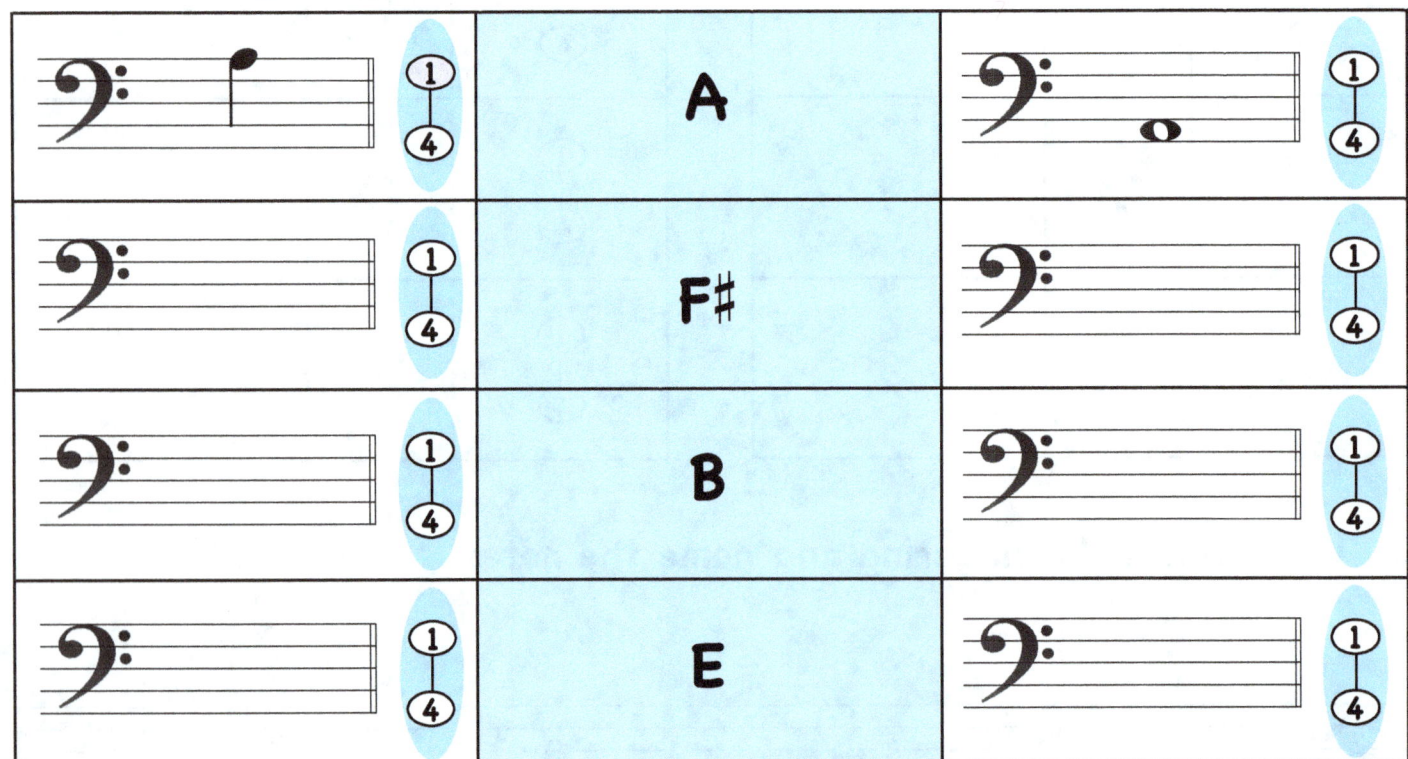

www.stringstastic.com   51

Name: _____   Date: _____

Test

TOTAL MARKS: _____/100

1. Name these notes. _____/12

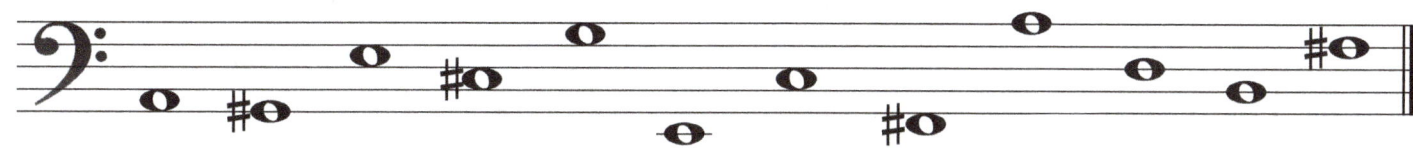

2. Label above each note in question 1 with the correct fingering.
   (0, 1, 4)   _____/12

3. How many beats are these notes? _____/12

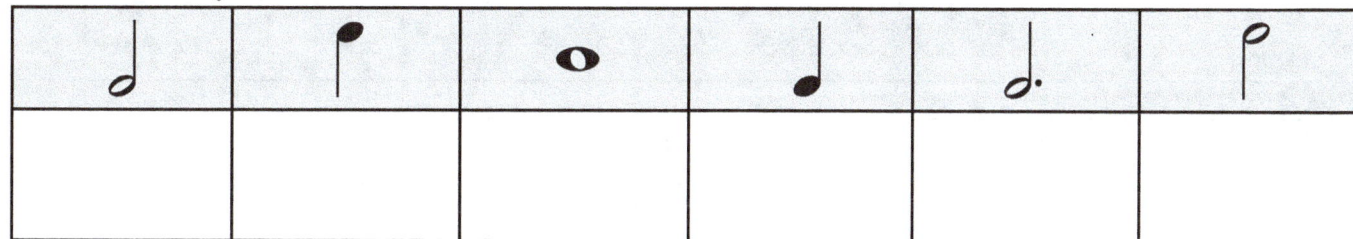

4. How many beats are these rests? _____/12

5. Complete each bar with one missing note. ♩ 𝅗𝅥 𝅗𝅥. 𝅝   _____/8

6. Complete each bar with one missing rest.   /8

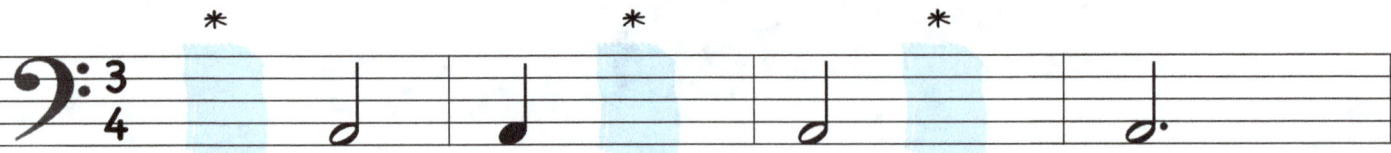
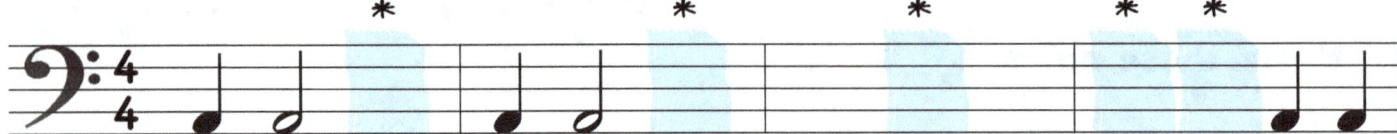

7. Write the beats and the time signature.   2/4 3/4 4/4   /20

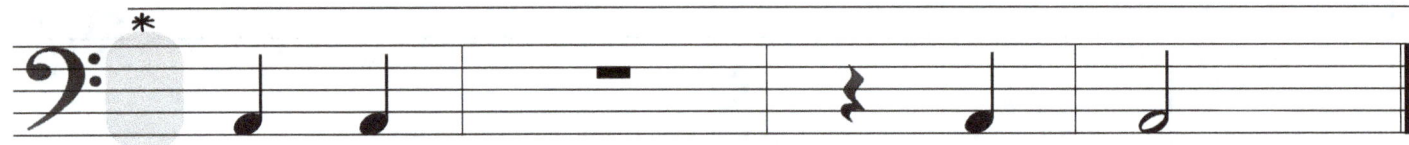
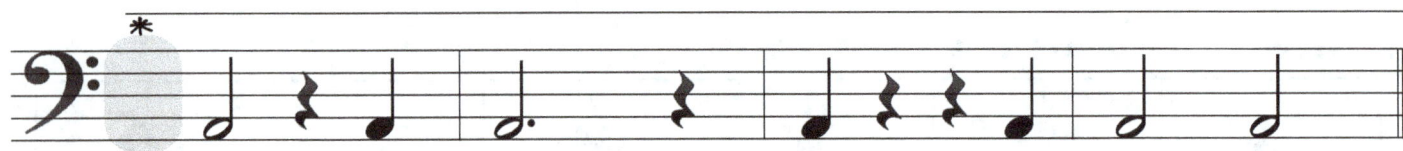

8. Fill in the two different fingerings for these notes and indicate the string they are on.   /16

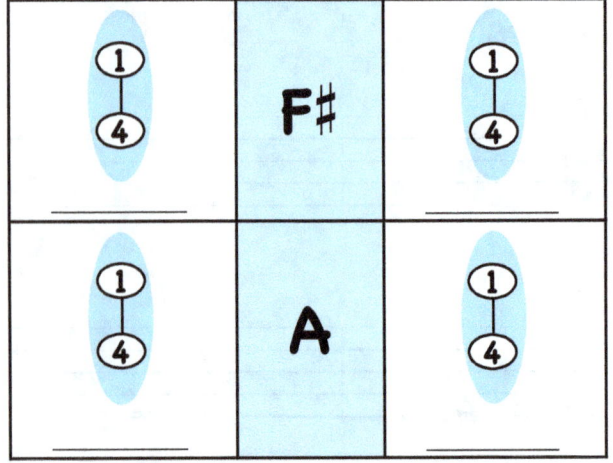